A CENTURY IN PHOTOGRAPHS

Published jointly by
Devon Federation of Women's Institutes
and Countryside Books

COUNTRYSIDE BOOKS
3 Catherine Road
Newbury, Berkshire

ISBN 1 85306 463 7

FRONT COVER PHOTOGRAPH OF BROADHEMBURY
SUPPLIED BY ANNE GILBERT, BROADHEMBURY W.I.

BACK COVER PHOTOGRAPH OF PERRY FARM, CHERITON FITZPAINE
SUPPLIED BY ELIZABETH FURZE, CHERITON FITZPAINE W.I.

PHOTOGRAPH ON PAGE 1 SHOWING TORQUAY IN THE 1950s,
FROM THE ROGER GRIMLEY COLLECTION

Designed by Graham Whiteman

Produced through MRM Associates Ltd., Reading

Printed by Woolnough Bookbinding Ltd., Irthlingborough

CONTENTS

Thomas Clapp's horse-bus arriving at Seaton. (Roger Grimley Collection)

FOREWORD

After the success of the County book, *Devon Within Living Memory*, about life in the 20th century, the Devon Federation of Women's Institutes welcomed the suggestion of a pictorial record of this very special part of the country. The photographs show how, over the years, so many aspects of Devon life have gone through change.

The one thing that has remained constant, however, is that Devon is a highly agricultural county with much of its population dependent on the land for its well-being.

As you look through this excellent book, you will see many photographs that will bring back memories and you will learn how things have moved on over the years.

Our thanks must go to the members who have kindly sent in the photographs enabling this book to be published; with special thanks once again to Mrs Pat Macdonald who has given up her time to co-ordinate all the information sent to us.

Ginny Addison-Smith
County Chairman

ACKNOWLEDGEMENTS

My thanks are due to all the Devon W.I. members who contributed their pictures and information. I should like to record my gratitude as well to the Cookworthy Museum at Kingsbridge, Mrs Sonia Gidal, Roger Grimley, and David James, who also by their generosity helped to make this most interesting publication possible; while Countryside Books made my task of co-ordination a great pleasure.

Pat Macdonald
Project Co-ordinator

5

INTO THE 20TH CENTURY

(1900 – 1919)

Queen Victoria was still on the throne when the century began and Devon was, as it remains today, a highly agricultural county with a rural economy heavily dependent on the land. The sea, too, has for centuries been the source of employment for many. Plymouth was, of course, an important naval base, and coastal towns and villages depended on fishing and seaborne trade for their livelihood.

Railways were largely responsible for the growth of one of Devon's main industries of the 20th century, for with the advent of this means of mass transport tourism had gathered momentum by 1900. Many country roads were little better than cart tracks, but the railways brought visitors into the county.

There has been great continuity over the century; for example the Thurlestone Hotel, near Kingsbridge, celebrated its centenary in 1996, having been for all that time in the ownership of the Grose family. In the early 1900s a modest village farmhouse providing accommodation in the remote South Hams, today is a four-star luxury hotel in a still small and unspoiled village. The golf course nearby celebrated its centenary in 1997.

Cottage homes were often isolated, the inhabitants dependent upon horse and cart, bicycle or their own feet to get about. Few people travelled far, relying on the carrier's cart for shopping 'in town'. Cars were for the wealthy, and the dust cloud accompanying a passing car in the summer would bring curious villagers to their door for a closer look.

Lighting was by candle or oil lamp, heating by open fire, and water came in a bucket from the well or stream. Life was physically very hard, and women's work in the home extremely arduous. In towns lamplighters still made their rounds at dawn and dusk, but in the country the night was unbroken by streetlamps or house lights.

Children walked to the all-age village schools, some good, some bad, and few had the opportunity or means for further education beyond the age of 12. Boys left school and started work on the land, in the mines and quarries, or on the sea the next day. Girls had little choice; going into service at the 'big house' was often their only chance of paid work. Many villages were still part of large estates, the local squire and parson having great influence on day to day life.

Sunday school outings and a day at the local fair were often the only chance to have a holiday. Men and women walked to hiring fairs to look for work.

Devon has forged close links with the armed forces, which remain unbroken today. In 1902 the foundation stone of the Royal Naval College at Dartmouth was laid by King Edward VII. Before the college opened all naval cadets trained aboard the training ship HMS *Britannia*. The Royal Navy's presence at Plymouth was all pervasive. In 1913 the RAF Mount Batten airfield opened as a Royal Naval Air Station. In the army, the Devonshire Regiment had a proud history; when the century opened Devonshire men were

fighting in the South African wars, and in 1914 there were volunteers in plenty for a fight that it was thought would be over by Christmas.

Every town and village in Devon suffered losses during the First World War, a sad time for many families. Although the fighting was far away, the war came home to those on the Devon coastline when German U-boats torpedoed shipping. In 1916 Devon's worst lifeboat disaster took place when 13 out of a crew of 15 were killed at Salcombe. With so many men away at the war, women were called on to take on 'men's work'. In 1918 women over 30 were given the vote for the first time (the rest had to wait until 1928).

The first Women's Institutes in Devon were formed in 1917 at Cullompton and Cornwood, women responding with new-found confidence to a desire to learn how to improve rural life, both for themselves and their families and for the wider community.

The Royal Standard Inn at Mary Tavy, 1910. It was so named after the inn supplied a meal for one of Queen Victoria's sons. (Mary Warne – Mary Tavy WI)

At Honiton market, 1912. The old pannier market has
long since been converted into shops.
(Nan Pearce – Stockland WI)

Below *Exton village c1912. The boys are standing on
what is now the busy and considerably widened A376
Exmouth to Exeter road. The boy on the left is holding a
hoop, a very popular toy on these quiet roads, while the
two on the right appear to have been sent to the village
shop with a small basket and a can for milk.* (Exton WI)

*Looking down Totnes High Street towards Fore Street in
1913. The shop fronts today are largely unchanged. The
Tudor East Gate arch was destroyed by fire in the early
1990s but has been rebuilt as an exact replica; the new
clock was given as a gift by the Borough of Kingston upon
Thames to replace the original.*
(Marjorie Pindard – Ipplepen WI)

Broadhembury has not changed much since this picture was
taken, with its many thatched cottages owned by the Drewe
family of Broadhembury House. Many cottages were built of
cob on a base of stone, thatched with long wheat straw.
(Anne Gilbert – Broadhembury WI)

Looking down on Brixham
harbour.
(Mr D. James – Brixham)

Proclaiming the fair at Barnstaple, September 1907,
preceded by the ancient custom of Toast and Ale in the
Guildhall, when spiced ale and toast were prepared for the
members of the Council and 'Barnstaple Fairing' for the
ladies. The three-day fair, one of the biggest in the West of
England for the sale of livestock, was officially declared
open at noon with the hoisting of a huge stuffed glove
from a window in the Guildhall.
(Margaret Hawkins – Pilton WI)

High Street, Ilfracombe during the coaching season, c1908.
Ilfracombe was a popular resort and one of the highlights
of a visit was a coach trip with either Colwill's or Thomas
Copp to Lynton, Hunters Inn, Sterridge Valley or

Woolacombe Sands and Shell Beach. The two concerns
competed strongly, each endeavouring to outdo the other
in smartness of turnout.
(Roger Grimley Collection)

From the message on the back of this postcard, it seems likely that this horse and carriage at Goodleigh was on its way back from Barnstaple Fair in 1906. In addition to the waggonette driver and passengers there seem to be several men from the New Inn, one still clutching his cider or beer pot.
(Roger Grimley Collection)

Below Waldon Hill and the Clock Tower, Torquay, c1907. This view shows three different types of transport: an early steam bus of the Torquay Road Car Company, an electric tram, and horse-drawn cabs.
(Roger Grimley Collection)

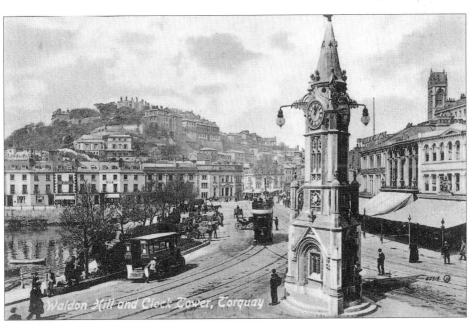

Waldon Hill and Clock Tower, Torquay

Butcher Charles Bond and his delivery van, c1918 at Aveton Gifford. His round took him to all the surrounding villages, and every year he had a photograph of the shop taken to be made into calendars for family and customers. He bought his first motorised van in the 1920s.
(Christine Scott – Diptford WI)

Frank and Elsie Sweetland, of Thorn Farm, Ottery St Mary with their three-wheeled car, 1910. Motoring was becoming more accessible, though the roads left much to be desired – Frank one night turned his car over in an encounter with a heap of stones.
(Mary Martin – Awliscombe WI)

Henry Gourd, carrier, outside Bishopsteignton church gates c1912. He began his career as a carrier in 1889 at the age of 12, conveying laundry between the residences in Teignmouth and the laundresses of his home village, Bishopsteignton. When he was called up for the war, his wife Thirza continued the business. (Roger Grimley Collection)

Workers at Pen slate quarry in the 1900s. The quarry is no longer open, though the remains of the old chimney can still be seen.
(Wendy Major – Ashburton WI)

A traction engine accident on Forches Hill, Sandford, 1912. Slow moving and reliable as they were for pulling heavy loads, little could stop them if they ran out of control. The driver of this engine was killed.
(Daphne Munday – Sandford WI)

A cheesemaking class at Town Barton, Sandford, 1916. Promoted by Sir William and Lady Ferguson Davie (seated front row) in an effort to encourage the making of cheese on local farms at a time when it was feared the art was under threat, this fortnight's class taught young women how to make Cheddar, Householder and other cheeses.
(Daphne Munday – Sandford WI)

The Stamp family scything a field near their home at Monkton in the early 1900s, with Dumpton Hill in the background. 'Grandfather Stamp', on the right, had six sons and was the local wheelwright. All his sons went off to fight in the First World War, and all came home safely.
(Irene Stuart – Awliscombe WI)

The Melhuish family of Wheddon Cross, tailors at work.
(Cissie Carpenter – Huntsham WI)

Below *Joe Elliott, local stonemason, standing in front of a wooden-doored recess which housed the village tap for Bantham's water supply. Each cottage had a key as all water had to be fetched, including that for the toilets 'out the back'. This was in use until 1931. Mr Elliott built many of the walls and church vaults and tombs in Thurlestone village.* (Kathleen Evans – Littleham WI)

Above *Women workers at the collar factory, Bideford Rope Walk, at the turn of the century. Women from Appledore walked the three miles there and back every day. The foreman kept a strict eye on his female workforce.*
(Shirley Hocking – Appledore WI)

The first committee of the new Cullompton Women's Institute – the first in Devon – in 1917. The president was the local doctor's wife, Mrs G. Gidley. At this time the women were all identified by their husbands – 'the bank manager's wife' etc. Since its inception the WI has helped women to achieve status in their own right.
(Muriel Coxhead – Cullompton WI)

Above The wedding at North Molton c1918 of Jack and Maud Westcott. They farmed at Higher Poole. One of the soldiers present was Jack's brother, just back from the war. Jack had a dry sense of humour; when they bought their first wireless set he remarked to another farmer at haymaking time, 'My wireless says 'tis gwain ter rain, what does yours say?' (Lucy Butt – Mortehoe WI)

Above The Tucker children and a pushchair-cum-toy of 1909. (Cissie Carpenter – Huntsham WI)

PETROCKSTOW WESLEYAN S.

Whitchurch school c1913, probably at harvest time. 'My family all went to this school; we walked a mile each way and had our pasties warmed by the coke stove.' The school is now closed and local children attend a new school closer to Tavistock. (Mary Warne – Mary Tavy WI)

Setting out on the Wesleyan Sunday school outing in 1909 from Petrockstowe. The destination was Westward Ho! 18 miles away. (Joan Hardwicke – Petrockstowe WI)

A very official looking group of policemen, but in fact they were in carnival dress for the Salcombe Carnival in 1908! The man in plain dress was M. William White, a draper of Fore Street and a town councillor. The Carnival is believed to be the forerunner of today's regatta.
(Audrey Howell – Stokenham Evening WI)

Below *The greasy pole at Aveton Gifford Regatta, July 1914. The barge giving support was normally used on the river Avon for transporting heavy goods such as coal or stone. Other events included a marathon foot race and horse racing. The regatta was restarted after the war but ceased c1930, to be revived in 1985 and become once again a popular local event.*
(Christine Scott – Diptford WI)

Harvest Festival celebrations at Dalwood Hill.
(Ella White – Dalwood WI)

This empty sand barge took families on boat trips up the river Taw at Barnstaple to the 'bar' where the river meets the sea. The group pictured in 1919 were all local people, possibly on a Baptist chapel outing. The river is now silted up. (Maragaret Hawkins – Pilton WI)

Bathing fashions c1912 at Dawlish.
(Marjorie Pindard – Ipplepen WI)

Left The Easterbrook family on Paignton beach, 1913; the pier in the background later burned down. (Eileen Wain – Stoke Gabriel WI)

Right Crowds in Exeter Street, North Tawton on George V's Coronation Day in 1911, following a procession led by the town band. There were sports and swings for the children, and a coronation tea. The ringers rang the church bells and the day ended with a bonfire at Hayne Hill.
(Kennedy Gregory – North Tawton WI)

The tea party held in the yard of Kelly House in 1902 to celebrate the coronation of Edward VII. A band came from Launceston to play for the festivities. The band consisted of Mr Clifford on the cornet, Mr Ham on the violin and Mr Peake on the double bass – they knew only two tunes, but these were repeated with great vigour all the afternoon and evening and everyone had a good time. (Marjorie Kelly – Kelly WI)

Above and Below Soldiers outside the Ring of Bells at
North Tawton, and 'out for the day' (the photographer
came from Okehampton). These were Devon Volunteers,
some time before the First World War in 1914.
(Kennedy Gregory – North Tawton WI)

Volunteers enlisting for the army at Salcombe, 1914, and about to leave town. There was no lack of men ready to join up in those early days.
(Cookworthy Museum, Kingsbridge)

A group of postmen and local people outside the post office at Stockland, 1914. On the walls are displayed posters identifying 'Types of the British Army'.
(Nan Pearce – Stockland WI)

BETWEEN THE WARS

⌇

(1920 – 1938)

Skirts and hair were shorter and the 'flapper' epitomised carefree youth in a period that brought great hardship to many. There were still older women in the long black Victorian dresses their own mothers had worn, but clothes were generally lighter and simpler. Hats were still essential wear for men, women and children.

Those who had given their lives during the war were not forgotten. Devon's county war memorial, made of Devon granite, was unveiled by the Prince of Wales outside Exeter Cathedral in 1921. Smaller ceremonies took place in every town and village.

Tradesmen began to change from horse and cart to motorised van. Car ownership spread and roads had to be improved. In 1920 the first car negotiated Clovelly's notorious main street. Trips by charabanc replaced the horse-drawn carriage or cart for outings, though passengers might still have to get out and walk on steep Devon hills. By 1938 the A38 between Exeter and Plymouth was already carrying over 3,000 vehicles a day.

The first tractors were threatening the role of horses on the land, but traditional ways still held good. Cider was being made on most farms. Names like Whiteways of Whimple became synonymous with Devon cider, and these family firms were active in encouraging farmers to improve their cider apple orchards for the future.

Times were changing at sea too, with sail trawlers being ousted by steam in the 1930s – soon to be superseded in turn by more powerful diesel engines.

Women could still be found, in villages like Beer, lacemaking while their men were away at sea. An Appledore man named Billy Rapson was a champion knitter of traditional Appledore jerseys, and even beat his own sister in a competition.

Renewal sometimes took the form of a return to a proud past. In 1928 the official title of Port was restored to Bideford. At Axminster, after 100 years, carpets were once again manufactured in the town.

From the early cat's-whisker to the 'modern' wireless, radio became our link with a wider world of music, drama, news and comedy. On the silver screen Garbo spoke and Al Jolson sang and the talkies tempted us to the cinema twice, sometimes three times, a week.

Heroines like Amy Johnson helped flying to enjoy a wave of popularity, and the airfield at Chivenor was opened for use by local clubs in 1934.

The Devon Federation of WIs was formed in 1920. From their earliest days, concerned to improve and protect rural life, Institutes campaigned for issues as var-

'The Home Barber', taken at Whitchurch in 1921. 'My grandfather used to cut his friends' hair whilst they were waiting to get their boots repaired by the cobbler next door.' (Mary Warne – Mary Tavy WI)

1920 – 1938

Iris Worden at Ashleigh Farm, Bridestowe, 1937. Classes in buttermaking were held by Devon County Council's agricultural committee to prepare students for the County Show. (Iris Pearn – Bridestowe WI)

ied as further education, school milk and dinners, widows' pensions, better standards of food hygiene, anti-litter laws and better care in childbirth. No one was better placed to understand the concerns of those living in the countryside.

Royal occasions during these years included the celebration of George V's Silver Jubilee in 1935 with sports, teas, fireworks and a mug each for all the children. Then we watched and listened as Edward VIII renounced his throne for the woman he loved, and the next year we joined in the celebrations for the coronation of George VI. And then there were rumours of war, Mr Chamberlain declared 'peace in our time', and Devon's soldiers and sailors began once again to prepare for conflict.

Bampton Fair c1920. Originally known as St Luke's Fair, this has been an annual event since the 1200s when it was primarily a sheep fair. By the 1800s horses and Exmoor ponies were the principal attractions. In 1985 livestock sales ceased and today the fair consists of the usual market, craft and amusement stalls. (Joyce Weston – Oakford WI)

The Modbury Harriers in the main street, 1920s. The Hunt is still active today with a traditional big meet each Boxing Day in Modbury.
(Christine Scott – Diptford WI)

Colyton's maypole dancers on their way to their next venue in 1923. The girls all wore laurel wreaths on their heads.
(Queenie Woollacott – Witheridge WI)

Bathing huts on Ilfracombe beach, 1924. The passion for sunbathing had not yet taken hold!
(Bobbie Maynard – Galmpton & Churston WI)

Buckerell school, near Honiton c1920. It consisted of one large room (with the three long windows) and a school house on either end. The inscription beside the main door read: 'Bring up a child in the way it should go and it will not depart from it.' The building was demolished c1960 for housing development.
(Betty Read – Awliscombe WI)

A fashionable bride in 1927 – Phyllis Perraton when she married Alfred Rogers at Dockwell.
(Christine Scott – Diptford WI)

Above At South Brent
gymkhana, 1920. The
event was held in a field
always known to locals as
'Harry Waters Lane'
though its official name
was Harwell Lane. It
ceased in the 1960s.
(Inez Jordan – South
Brent WI)

The Whitchurch
bellringers' outing c1920
(Mary Warne – Mary Tavy
WI)

Beer Primary School lacemaking class in the 1920s. The girl bottom left is May Wakley, who became a well known lacemaker and teacher. Only a decade or so ago Beer had been at the centre of the hand-made 'Honiton lace' industry, but the contest with man-made fibres and machinery could not be won. The skills were still passed down, however, and today there is great interest again in this intricate art.
(May Wakley – Beer WI)

Haymaking at Norton, near Dartmouth, 1927. Horses were still providing the power on the land. (Joyce Hutchings – Dartmouth WI)

Mary Driver lacemaking outside her home in Fore Street, Beer. The women of the village often worked outdoors during summer, and were happy to earn extra pence by posing for photographs. Many of Mary's descendants still live in Beer, including May Wakley.
(May Wakley – Beer WI)

Mamie Lock knitting the traditional Appledore Jersey (referred to as a 'frock'), with special worsted yarn. Each knitter had their own special pattern on the shoulder, which acted as a form of identification. The jerseys became the trademark of the Appledore deep sea sailors.
(Shirley Hocking – Appledore WI)

William Rogers sawing timber near Totnes in the early 1920s. The old steam engine provides the power for the job.
(Mary Rogers – Sparkwell WI)

Official opening of Burrator Reservoir – originally built in the 1890s and then enlarged between 1923 and 1928; the stone was laid in 1925. The reservoir supplied Plymouth with water.
(Beryl Dark – Meavy & Sheepstor WI)

The Lang family off to market in the 1920s. The ladies would be driven the mile and a half to Waytown Cross on the Clovelly to Bideford road, where they caught the Hartland bus which dropped them off at the Bideford pannier market. (Jessie Skinner – Petrockstowe WI)

The fishmonger's shop run in Dartmouth by the Fleet family. The barrels outside the shop contained salt fish, a common item in the diet before the days of easy preservation methods. (Irene Fleet – Dartmouth WI)

BETWEEN THE WARS (1920–1938)

East Street, Ashburton with a mixture of horse-drawn and motorised traffic. Only one building has changed since this photo was taken, with a bank built at the corner of St Lawrence Lane. (Wendy Major – Ashburton WI)

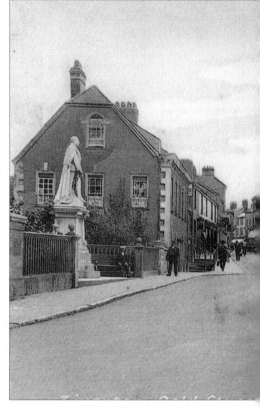

Below *Brixham fishermen and their catch.* (Mr D. James – Brixham)

Gold Street, Tiverton. This was probably the busiest street in the town between the wars, as access to the town centre, the railway and the buses lay along it. When the train and bus stations were moved, the street changed completely, and it was made one-way in the 1970s, with the trade of some of the shops suffering as a result. (Ginny Addison-Smith – Halberton WI)

Below Torquay Promenade and Abbey Sands in the 1930s, overlooked by the Palm Court Hotel. The absence of road traffic is remarkable. (Roger Grimley Collection)

BETWEEN THE WARS (1920–1938)

Exeter City Fire Brigade in the early 1930s, with their newly delivered Dennis machine. The whole city was covered by this very small force, who all lived in the eight houses at Danes Castle. (Ann Andrews – Awliscombe WI)

Teignmouth lifeboat on Lifeboat Day 1939. This boat had no engine but was manned by tough local oarsmen. On the annual Lifeboat Day a maroon was fired, the crew assembled, the lifeboat was launched and a practice row would ensue. Today Teignmouth has a fast modern boat called an 'Atlantic 21'. (Lady Palmer – Withleigh WI)

The kitchen of a typical Dartmoor longhouse – Ensworthy Farm at Gidleigh – in 1939, showing the open hearth and the use of bellows to keep the fire alight. Mrs Mabel Hill is sitting on the wooden settle (not very comfortable!) and to the right is the 'modern' range, also used for cooking. The floor was of flagstones.
(Gwen Bowles – Exminster WI)

J.C. 'Coey' Webber in 1930, blacksmith at Chevithorne until he retired in 1948. A smith all his working life, he started as an apprentice in Minehead.
(Barbara Hill – Chevithorne & Bolham WI)

Getting the horses ready for a day's work on the farm c1930.
(Betty Goodman – Stokenham WI)

Threshing corn at Kersdown Barton, Bampton, 1938, and a break for refreshments.
(Joyce Weston – Oakford WI)

This Chevrolet bus belonging to Gourds was en route to Teignmouth in the mid 1930s when it was struck by a clay lorry. Miraculously no one was hurt.
(Roger Grimley Collection)

Petrockstowe church outing in 1930. The charabanc was still popular for group transport – the hood at the back could be pulled over if it rained.
(Joan Hardwicke – Petrockstowe WI)

Above Schoolchildren setting out from Dawlish station on an outing in the early 1930s. The station is still open today, though with far fewer trains. (Win Aggett – Dawlish WI)

The presentation of Jubilee mugs at Lamerton, Tavistock in 1935, to commemorate George V's Silver Jubilee. Mr George Veale, then aged 86, is presenting mugs donated by Mr and Mrs Brown who kept the village store. (Rosie Farleigh – Stokenham Evening WI)

An evocative photo of childhood in the 1930s – Dalwood boys' cricket team in 1934. (Ella White – Dalwood WI)

Crowds turned out to greet King Edward VIII in Tavistock in 1936. As Duke of Cornwall he had been a frequent visitor on Duchy business. A year later, the Abdication over, celebrations went ahead for the Coronation of George VI.
(Mary Warne – Mary Tavy WI)

Mr George Huddy, an employee of Whiteways of Whimple, grafting an apple tree in the 1930s, with his Jack Russell 'Tiny' in the tree.
(Mary Burrough – Whimple WI)

Spraying cider apple trees in the 1930s at Whimple, using one of the earliest machines.
(Mary Burrough – Whimple WI)

THE SECOND WORLD WAR

(1939 – 1945)

On Sunday morning, 3rd September 1939, Prime Minister Chamberlain announced that we were at war with Germany. For a while it seemed a 'phoney war', but the early summer of 1940 brought the evacuation from Dunkirk and then the Battle of Britain fought over southern England, and the war became terribly real.

Never had the civilian population been so involved in a war. We criss-crossed windows with sticky tape against blasts, shaded car headlights and blacked out light from our homes. Signposts and station name plates were removed to confuse the enemy. Church bells were silenced for the duration, their sound meaning only that the invader had landed. Air raid shelters were issued – an Anderson for the garden or a Morrison for the house. Gas masks had to be carried everywhere, even by the smallest child. Iron railings and saucepans went to make Spitfires – or so they said. Ration books, queues, shortages, making do, digging for victory, we endured them all. Women's Institutes did their bit, helping women to learn new skills and cope with responsibilities and, most memorably, ensuring that nothing went to waste as they jammed, pickled, bottled and canned in answer to the government's plea not to waste a single fruit or vegetable.

The airfields at Chivenor and Mount Batten were taken over by the RAF, the latter becoming a major base for flying boats.

Plymouth suffered its first major air raid in March 1941, when much of the old city centre was destroyed outright. Raids continued through April and nearly 600 people died. It became one of the most heavily bombed cities in England, a sign of how important this great port was in the war effort. Charles Church, bomb damaged, was left in ruins after the war as a memorial to all those who died in the city.

Exeter was bombed in April 1942 and a daylight raid followed in late December the same year. Over 250 people were killed and many ancient buildings destroyed, with the main High Street gutted and damage to the cathedral. Teignmouth was another town to suffer, this time from 'tip and run' raids that left over 200 buildings destroyed and nearly 80 dead. At St Marychurch, Babbacombe, 26 children and their teachers died when the church was bombed.

People did their bit for the war effort in the Home Guard, the ARP, the Fire Service, the ambulance service, the Women's Voluntary Service, the Women's Land Army, and so many more. Firewatching became a normal part of working life, and the skill of the stirrup pump was employed on many nights when incendiary bombs rained down.

Some areas of Devon were quieter, and provided homes for evacuees from the heavily bombed towns and cities of the county and from as far away as London. It was sometimes a culture shock for both sides, and there are inevitably stories of hardship and unhappiness, but in many cases friendships were made which lasted well beyond the ending of the war.

After Pearl Harbor brought America into the war, US troops became a familiar

1939 – 1945

sight in the county. 'Any gum, chum?' became the catchphrase of children eager to sample the delights of sweets and chocolate, and the Americans' generosity was soon legendary. Close links were forged between them and local communities, links which have stood the test of time and are still strong today.

Late in 1943 a group of villages on and near the coast to the north-east of Kingsbridge was requisitioned by the Army and evacuated of all their 3,000 civilian inhabitants. Here rehearsals took place for the D-Day landings by US troops. On 4th June 1944 that hard-fought practice was made reality when an armada of US and British troops left Dartmouth harbour to become the left wing of the invasion forces in Normandy. Later that year the first inhabitants of those villages were allowed to return, but despite government compensation the damage and decay was such that many people never came back to their homes to live.

The coming of peace in May 1945 was celebrated with bonfires, dances and street parties all over Devon. Hoarded treats were produced and shared so that the children could enjoy a wonderful day, and once again the church bells were allowed to ring out.

The Plymouth wartime ambulance service used any vehicle that would hold a stretcher. This 'ambulance' in October 1939 was a removal van with a framework to hold four stretchers. The unit station was in Princess Square. (Marjorie Ricketts – Bickleigh WI)

THE SECOND WORLD WAR (1939–1945)

Bampton Home Guard on the march. After a day's work they would be ready to stand guard against invasion.
(Joyce Weston – Oakford WI)

Below Inspection of Kingsbridge Home Guard c1940, soon after their formation. They kept a nightly watch for invasion forces from Churchstow church tower, a local vantage point with visibility for many miles. Their HQ was at the old school in Duncombe Street, Kingsbridge. One of their jobs was to guard the estuary up to Salcombe, where they worked in liaison with the Army.
(Barbara Wills – Dawlish WI)

'George, in his newly issued uniform, at Plymouth.' The wartime fire service was in the front line, particularly in Plymouth where they faced great danger almost nightly during the blitz. (Marjorie Ricketts – Bickleigh WI)

Topsham Special Constables, 1940. (Jean Binding – Topsham WI)

THE SECOND WORLD WAR (1939–1945)

Civil Defence personnel at Barton Hall, Torquay.
(Mary Boon – Meavy & Sheepstor WI)

Below *Castle Street telephone exchange, Exeter, during the war. During the bombing of the city staff went on to the exchange roof to deal with incendiary bombs which were falling all around. Many adjoining buildings were destroyed but this action by the staff helped to save the exchange.*
(Joan Galpin – Estuary WI)

Right Queen Elizabeth inspecting servicewomen at the Flagstaff Steps, Devonport. These were 'Boating Wrens' at Devonport Dockyard, trained to take charge of small RN boats to release the men to go to sea. Flagstaff Steps was the HQ of 'Captain D' (Destroyers) and his staff. (Lady Palmer – Withleigh WI)

Elsie Newton of Down Thomas obtained a bus conductor's licence in 1939, at the age of 22. She worked on her father's bus service and one small boy's reaction to seeing a female conductor for the first time was, 'Oh, look, a lady be the ticket man!' The fish fryers in Ebrington Street, Plymouth would make up a special pack of fish and chips and these would be packed round the engine to keep them warm until the end of the journey where the servicemen stationed at Heybrook Bay would be waiting. (Roger Grimley Collection)

'I worked in service as a cook. After I married my soldier fiance in 1941, he suggested I apply for Post Office work, which I did and got paid £3 5s a week. I worked as a postwoman in Exmouth from 1941 to 1946.'
(Kathleen Evans –Littleham WI)

Above Filling sandbags at a local farm just before war was declared.
(Avril Williams – Broadhembury WI)

On this Dartmoor farm at Gidleigh, the children were helping farmer Jim Hill dig the potatoes, one row at a time. The children would pick up the potatoes and put them into the special baskets.
(Gwen Bowles – Exminster WI)

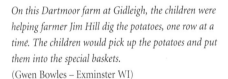

Despite the increasing use of machinery on the farm, in many places horses still provided the power. Cutting corn with a binder at Parkham in the early 1940s, with Wyndom Lang holding the horses and William Lang on the binder. (Jessie Skinner – Petrockstowe WI)

Below *A self binder at Washbourne Barton, Harbertonford in 1940. (Peggy Scott – Manaton WI)*

Land girls picking apples in Royds Orchard, Charleton. The apples were sacked, loaded and taken to Bonds cider factory (now closed) in Kingsbridge. (Jane Horswill – Kingsbridge)

Several official photographs were taken at Ralph Hoare's Mount Barten Farm by the Ministry of Information, intended to show how farming life was adapting successfully to the challenges of the war. This one shows the pay parade, mid-day on Saturday, with Robert Hoare paying William Goss.
(Barbara Bradburn – Broadhempston WI)

Opposite *Women are among the workers in the spoil from the Hemerdon Mine, opened up for wolfram (or tungsten) during the war. From the back, l. to r., are George Lee, Gwen Clemo, Audrey Wilcocks, Florrie Mudge, Joyce Allen, Marjorie Jones, Amy Underwood, Doris Higman, Joan Tucker and Ernest Reed.*
(Florrie Mudge – Sparkwell WI)

The Children's Carnival at Dawlish, 1941. This was an annual event, the children leading the procession through the town, preceded by the band. Young Miss Selley's costume (centre) was made from an old army uniform and was later used by several children in subsequent fancy dress events and always won prizes! (Rose Selley – Starcross WI)

Two little evacuees from London in 1940. They returned home after the first raid on Exeter. The boy's house was destroyed by bombing during the war but no one was hurt. (Beryl Kingman – Pebbleford WI)

THE SECOND WORLD WAR (1939–1945)

Right and opposite The aftermath of the blitz on Plymouth city centre in 1941.
(Devon Record Office)

Below Bomb damage to Aveton Gifford church – a late 13th century church almost completely destroyed by a 'tip and run' bombing raid in mid-1943. It was rebuilt after the war.
(Christine Scott – Diptford WI)

American troops helping with the evacuation in 1943; Mr F. Blank leaving his home in Slapton.
(Cookworthy Museum, Kingsbridge)

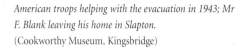

Below Late in 1943 a group of villages adjacent to and on the coast north-east of Kingsbridge was requisitioned and 3,000 civilian inhabitants were evacuated so that rehearsals for the D-Day landings could be held by US troops.
(Pat Macdonald – Thurlestone WI)

IMPORTANT MEETINGS

The area described below is to be REQUISITIONED urgently for military purposes, and must be cleared of its inhabitants by DECEMBER 20th, 1943.

Arrangements have been made to help the people in their moves, to settle them elsewhere, and to advise and assist them in the many problems with which they will be faced. To explain these arrangements

PUBLIC MEETINGS

will be held as follows:

FRIDAY 11 a.m. **EAST ALLINGTON CHURCH**
Nov. 12th 2-30 p.m. **STOKENHAM CHURCH**

Earl Fortescue, M.C., The Lord Lieutenant in the Chair.

SATURDAY 11 a.m. **BLACKAWTON CHURCH**
Nov. 13th 2-30 p.m. **SLAPTON VILLAGE HALL**

Sir John Daw, J.P., Chairman Devon County Council in the Chair.

These general meetings will be immediately followed by special meetings to discuss the problems of farmers, who are requested to remain behind for them.

IT IS VITALLY IMPORTANT to every householder that he should arrange to attend whichever of these meetings is nearest to his home, and where necessary employers of labour are requested to give their work-people time off for this purpose.

THE AREA AFFECTED

ALL LAND AND BUILDINGS lying within the line from the sea at the east end of Blackpool Bay in Stoke Fleming parish to Bowden ; thence northward along the road to the Sportsman's Arms ; thence west along the Dittisham-Halwell road to the cross-roads 1-mile east of Halwell village ; from this cross-road along the road to the Kingsbridge road to the Woodleigh-Buckland cross-roads ; thence along the road Buckland, Frogmore, Bessands. The roads forming the boundary are outside the area.

The parishes involved are the whole, or almost the whole, of Blackawton, East Allington, Sherford, Slapton and Strete, most of Stokenham, and parts of Stoke Fleming, Buckland-tout-Saints and Halwell.

57

At the St Giles in the Wood Carnival, near Torrington, in 1945, Judith Chamings leading Jenny the donkey, with her sister Pamela and cousin Hazel Chope in the cart.
(Judith Domleo – Atherington & Umberleigh WI)

Above and right *A civic welcome for incoming US troops in 1943, with a parade at Mayflower Steps on the Plymouth Barbican.*
(Devon Record Office)

Below *VE celebrations varied from huge community street parties to those arranged amongst a few neighbours and friends, as here in May Street, Exeter in June 1945.*
(Beryl Kingman – Pebbleford WI)

Top right *In 1945, on the green, Mrs Westall, wife of the then vicar of Shaldon, presenting wallets to servicemen from the village who had served in the war.*
(Lady Palmer – Withleigh WI)

Right *A Victory party at Sidmouth, 1945.*
(Margaret Tucker – Sandford WI)

THE POST-WAR YEARS

(1946 – 1959)

*I*t seemed a long while before we could finally put the war behind us. Food rationing continued for several more years – bread came off ration in 1948 and children could at last buy as many sweets as they liked in 1953. We entered a nuclear age, but coal stayed on ration until 1958!

The freezing winter of 1947 seemed to epitomise life at the time – rather bleak and a day by day struggle to keep well fed and warm. But change was on the way. Dior's 'New Look' was a breath of feminity and frivolity, and as the 1950s wore on the 'teenager' was created and music, dance and entertainment were never the same again.

Bomb damage took many years to erase and the opportunity was taken to build modern shopping centres in places like Plymouth and Exeter. It all took time; the church at Aveton Gifford which was bombed in 1943 was not reconsecrated until 1957.

The post-war government presided over the creation of the Welfare State, and the new National Health Service saw the end of the doctor's bill and the workhouse infirmary.

Further education was becoming available to all young people and in 1955 full university status was granted to what was the University College of the South West at Exeter.

Every peacetime summer since the 1920s, the School Specials were seen on the county's railways – several carriages attached to the normal rolling stock and filled with children going to the seaside. Rounders and cricket, sand castles and tea made a day to remember, before the homeward journey with sand-filled shoes.

People started taking holidays again after the war, and Devon was a favourite destination for an increasingly mobile population. Exmoor was designated a National Park in 1954. In 1959 the first motorway in England opened and in Devon increasing concern was being felt at the growth of traffic on the county's narrow roads.

Change was felt in the Armed Forces too, and as cutbacks spread the Devonshire Regiment was absorbed into the newly formed Devonshire and Dorset Regiment in 1954.

On the land small self-supporting family farms continued as they always had. At Wadhayes, Awliscombe the same family had farmed since 1900. They kept a herd of pedigree Devons, sent the milk to Hemyock Dairies and reared and sold the young bulls. Corn, beans, kale, mangolds, swede and turnips were grown; hay and silage were made; cider was made and drunk at most meals, the surplus apples going to Whiteways at Whimple; ewes lambed and pigs were reared and sold as 'porkers' or 'baconers'; poultry was free range; apples, pears, plums, soft fruit of all kinds, rhubarb and filbert nuts were grown and harvested; anything surplus was bottled or jammed.

Horses were losing the contest with machinery on the farms, but ploughing matches continued to be popular places to compare notes. Cheriton & District Ploughing Association was formed in 1945

1946 – 1959

nd had several distinguished ploughmen in its memberships including Mr John Nott, British Isles Champion.

A disaster that made news round the world was the flood that devastated Lynmouth on the night of Friday, 15th August 1952. Over 90 million tons of water surged down the valley from the hills and moors, leaving 34 people dead, 93 buildings destroyed and 28 bridges down. Other villages such as Parracombe, Oxford, and Brendon also endured a night of terror. There were many awards later made for the rescue work done that night, including a George Medal for PC D. Harper of the Devon Constabulary, only 24 years old and a constable for just 16 months.

Television was seen by many people for the first time on Coronation Day, when friends and neighbours crowded in to watch the historic occasion on the very few sets then in use. The Coronation of Queen Elizabeth II gave us all a much needed boost in June 1953, with parades, street parties and bonfires all over Devon – it was time to look forward to a new Elizabethan Age.

Princess Alexandra at the County Show in Whipton in 1956, when for the first time since the war butter was made at the show. The Princess is looking at the Devon Young Farmers' exhibit. (Jean Underdown – Colyton WI)

THE POST-WAR YEARS (1946–1959)

The cold winter of 1947 at Moretonhampstead, the streets deserted. Heavy snow fell in February for about ten days. 'My husband was at the time at Seale Agricultural College and his was one of the first cars to get out. He used Land Army girls as ballast, dropping them off en route. The thaw eventually came but froze again, proving disastrous for evergreen trees – the weight of the ice split them. Skating and tobogganing were the popular entertainments.' (Peggy Scott – Manaton WI)

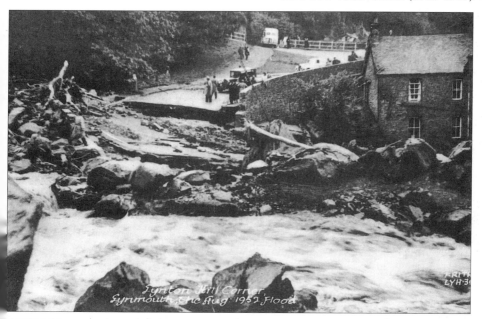

Left *The hunt meet at Diptford c1950. Mr and Mrs Norman were the last licensees of the Rising Sun pub and their daughter Everal is passing drinks round the Dart Vale Harriers. This was one of the last meets before the pub closed. The Harriers themselves are now amalgamated with the South Pool Harriers.*
(Christine Scott – Diptford WI)

Above *Part of the destruction caused at Lynmouth by the floods in August 1952, the road washed away by the strength of the river.*
(Roger Grimley Collection)

Below *Kingsbridge Quay in the late 1940s. Since then the head of the small quay has been altered to provide a pleasant town square complete with bandstand, and improved but much more extensive car parking. At the opposite end of the quay there is now a sports centre and by the millennium the long awaited swimming pool should be built.*
(Christine Scott – Diptford WI)

Starcross to Exemouth Ferry.

The Starcross to Exmouth ferry. A ferry was running here in the 12th century. South Devon Railway acquired the ferry in 1848 and it provided an excellent link between Exmouth and Starcross; it was later taken over by the Devon Dock & Steamship Company and in 1981 it passed into private ownership. Today it runs during the summer only. (Ruby Cumes – Starcross WI)

A summer morning at Liverton in the late 1950s and the ladies of the village set off to shop in Newton Abbot. Every journey was a chance to 'have a natter' and when villagers were telling each other bits of gossip they would say: 'I heard it on Potter's bus.' (Roger Grimley Collection)

Huntsham post office in 1956, with Mrs C. Davis, the postmistress for many years. On the left is Bob Carpenter with the postbag full, ready to start a mile round to outlying farms, and on the right is Mr Vinney who brought the post by van from Tiverton main office at 7.30 am.
(Cissie Carpenter – Huntsham WI)

__Right__ Judith and Pamela Chamings on Saunton Sands in 1953.
(Judith Domleo – Atherington & Umberleigh WI)

The staff of the Gaumont Cinema, North Street, Exeter c1950, with the manager flanked by twelve usherettes, four commissionaires, cleaners, office staff and the projectionists at the back. The cinema opened Whit Monday 1932 with a film called Sunshine Susie *– the Wurlitzer organ was later badly damaged during the wartime bombing. The cinema became a bingo hall in 1963.*
(Hilda Ogg – Bradninch WI)

Amateur dramatics was very popular, even in smaller communities. The Ghost Train *was an ambitious project for the Sandford Players in 1953, produced by Peter and Gordon Vasey and with a cast of 14. (Daphne Munday – Sandford WI)*

Kingsbridge St John Ambulance nurses treat a casualty, to great amusement, at Kingsbridge School sports day c1950. (Barbara Wills – Dawlish WI)

A land girl crowned Harvest Queen at Moretonhampstead Carnival in 1946. Later that year the land girls left the hostel in Court Street they had occupied during and since the war, and the Land Army was finally disbanded in October 1950. Many of the girls married local men and some remained working on the land. (Peggy Scott – Manaton WI)

The famous ox roast at Lapford took place for several years in the early 1950s, raising funds for the church restoration. People came from miles around to the field behind the church where the bungalows in Orchard Close now stand. Traditionally, one of the oldest residents, Eliza Horwell, known as Granny, cut the first slice, which was then auctioned and always raised a fair amount. Pictured are local butchers Harry Sanders and Jack Gale, who supervised the cooking, with George Tucker turning the spit handle. (Margaret Tucker – Sandford WI)

Modbury Young Farmers' Club horse-judging at Widland Farm, 1948. Many parents supported it and allowed their farms and animals to be used for stock judging, sheep shearing etc. Modbury YFC has now closed, after thriving for 45 years. (Christine Scott – Diptford WI)

Farmers at Modbury Market in July 1948, with Jack Cockran selling calves.
(Mary Rogers – Sparkwell WI)

Killing the pig at Lower Tale Farm, Payhembury c1950. Jim Daniel and the butcher, Mr Turner, are shaving the pig before it is gutted and hung. Food was still rationed after the war and when a pig was killed on the farm, meat points were deducted from the ration books.
(Jean Underdown – Colyton WI)

THE POST-WAR YEARS (1946–1959)

Mrs Amy Carpenter of Huntsham on washday in 1957 – outside with the washtub in the days before washing machines. Mrs Carpenter is now over 100 years old.
(Cissie Carpenter – Huntsham WI)

Left *Mrs Beatrice Pille, and helpers, at White Cross Farm, taking cream and milk from the churn c1958. Cream was made here every day and she took her produce to Exeter market.*
(Elizabeth Furze – Cheriton Fitzpaine WI)

An evening class on lampshade making at Huntsham – a very necessary new skill to be learned before electricity came to the village in 1957.
(Margaret Thomas – Huntsham WI)

The Luxton family and friends taking a teabreak from haymaking at Plainsfield, Withleigh in 1951.
(June Luxton – Withleigh WI)

After harvesting, the corn was not always threshed and baled in the field; sometimes it was brought up near to the house, built into a stack and threshing took place there at a later time. The base of the stack being built at High Grange, Dalwood, 1952.
(Elsa Chapman – Dalwood WI)

John Blackmore with the last working horses at Twitcham Farm, West Down in 1950. He used working horses all his farming days and retired in 1955. 'We usually kept between two and four working horses; sometimes three would be used when harvesting corn with a self-binding machine, and two were needed for many tasks.' Tractors gradually replaced horses after 1945.
(Margaret Thomas – West Down WI)

Below *An early combine harvester at John Chamings' farm at South Healand, St Giles in the Wood, near Torrington in the late 1940s. The combining was done by agricultural contractors James Murch & Sons of Little Torrington. Mechanising the corn harvest greatly reduced the manpower needed and the hard physical labour involved.*
(Judith Domleo – Atherington & Umberleigh WI)

The whole family could help in the fields at haymaking time – 1955 at Ritson Farm, Halwell.
(Peggy Scott – Manaton WI)

73

A street party at Kingsbridge, organised by the residents of Wallingford Road to celebrate the Coronation of Queen Elizabeth II in 1953. (Barbara Wills – Dawlish WI)

Left *Tuckenhay cider store in the late 1940s. Cider was made from local apples and until the late 1950s it was brought to Tuckenhay by horse and cart. Later, as the orchards were dug up, apple juice was imported from France but the quality was not as high and the whole enterprise was closed down by the 1970s, when the cider store was turned into luxury flats and houses. (Sheila Johnson – Ashprington WI)*

The Floral Dance at Dawlish on Coronation Day 1953. The then Mayor of Dawlish, Mr Eveleigh, led the dancers through the town headed by music relayed on loudspeakers from a lorry. (Rose Selley – Starcross WI)

THE SIXTIES AND SEVENTIES

(1960 – 1979)

The winter of 1963 will long be remembered. As quickly as roads were cleared they were blocked again by snow and in many rural areas it was several months before minor roads were opened. In late spring in some areas, impacted snow and ice had to be drilled off the pavements.

Dr Beeching's axe fell on the railways during the early 1960s. Many branch lines, of which Devon had a good number, were closed, a sad end to the children's Seaside Specials. Roads, on the other hand, improved beyond recognition compared with only a few decades before. The river Tamar forms, for a great part of its length, a natural boundary between Devon and Cornwall. In 1962 the Queen opened the new Saltash suspension road bridge which runs over the river parallel to Brunel's railway bridge. From the early 1970s the new M5 provided easy access to the county from the north, and relieved traffic congestion around Exeter. Smaller roads continued to suffer, though, from the pressure of increasingly heavy lorries and sheer number of cars. Back streets built in the days of the horse and cart were clogged by parked cars.

Rural transport systems declined and many Devonians living in outlying villages found that a car was an essential means of transportation. Supermarkets revolutionised the way we shop, and corner and village shops found it hard to compete. The abolition of the eleven-plus examination and building of comprehensive schools led to the closure of many small village schools. The school leaving age was raised to 16.

The music, behaviour and dress of the young became a matter of perplexity to their elders. The age of majority was reduced in 1968 from 21 to 18 years. Television and private telephones were to be found in most homes, and only in the most rural areas were the 'mod cons' of electricity, indoor sanitation and running water unavailable. Concorde made her maiden flight in 1969, and the same year man reached the moon.

In 1960 we said goodbye to the farthing, our smallest British coin, and in 1971 decimal currency swept away the old shillings, sixpences, threepences, florins, half-crowns and halfpennies as well. In 1973 we joined the European Economic Community. For some time in the 1970s Devon's fishing industry received a boost as international restrictions fell on other traditional fishing grounds, but it was not to be long before we too felt the effects of international policies.

A national outbreak of foot and mouth disease in cattle brought ruin on some farmers. No animals were allowed to be moved and farms affected were quarantined, the diseased animals slaughtered on the spot.

The Queen visited Plymouth in Royal Silver Jubilee Year, 1977. 'I had waited hours to get this shot, sitting on a hired folding chair from early morning. (Inez Jordan – South Brent WI)

1960 – 1979

Celebrating the Queen's Silver Jubilee in 1977. On the ladder Hedley Luxton and David Britton, and l. to r. Len Christopher, Clifford Orchard, Fred Britton, Mark Christopher, Gerald Luxton, Percy Crook, Kevin Luxton, Stanley Britton and Ernest Luxton. (June Luxton – Withleigh WI)

The need actively to protect our beautiful countryside was increasingly recognised. In 1964 Braunton Burrows was declared a National Nature Reserve, one of the largest areas of sand dunes in Britain, with many wild flowers and rare sea and marsh birds to be found there. The Devon Federation of WIs celebrated its 50th anniversary in 1970 by purchasing a part of the South Devon coastline at Sugary Cove, near Dartmouth, and presenting it to the National Trust.

The construction of the Tamar Road Bridge, started in 1959, was complete by 1962 and it was opened by the Queen. It runs parallel to Isambard Kingdom Brunel's rail bridge over the Tamar but is now proving inadequate at peak holiday times. (Marjorie Ricketts – Bickleigh Plymouth WI)

Bottom left and left

*Floods in December 1960
caused great damage to the
Trout Inn, Bickleigh and
other property in the area.
Also shown is a
waterlogged Leat Street,
Tiverton.*
(Hilda Gormley –
Bickleigh Tiverton WI)

*The 1963 winter blizzards
– the first vehicle through
with supplies of milk, at
Devils Elbow Bend on the
main road from Plymouth
to Princetown.
Communities were cut off
for days at a time,
sometimes for weeks.
Bread was baked in
Dartmoor Prison in two-
foot loaves which were cut
in half to be sold locally.*
(Beryl Dark – Meavy &
Sheepstor WI)

Beating the bounds, 1960. Residents of Bridestowe and
Sourton Common, Dartmoor taking part in the ceremony,
a walk round the seven-mile perimeter of the common,
beating each boundary stone with a stick. It takes place
every seven years, and is a traditional means of ensuring
youngsters remember where the boundary markers lie.
The Commoners' Association formed early this century
represents farmers who use the moor and helps to define
and control the management of common land and its
grazing rights. (Iris Pearn – Bridestowe WI)

Below *Hatherleigh cattle market c1960; Gordon Vick and son David the auctioneers. J. Gordon Vick came to the West Country in the 1930s and built up a business whose annual turnover in the 1990s is over £12 million. Hatherleigh is a weekly market and provides a focal point for the area.* (Chrissie Mayne – Bratton Clovelly WI)

Right *Bringing in hay bales by tractor at Horsebrook, Avonwick, 1960s, with Rodney Hooker driving a Ferguson tractor for Neil Scott. On the load is Roger Poyntz-Roberts who beame YF organiser for Devon and then went to New Zealand.* (Christine Scott – Diptford WI)

Bill Horn, owner of the m/v Enterprise, began running trips round Exmouth bay in 1948 in summer, and went fishing and trawling in the winter.
(Peggy Horn – Withycombe Raleigh WI)

Left *March 5th 1966 was the last day trains ran on the branch line Seaton Junction-Colyton-Colyford-Seaton. 'My husband told the time by the trains on this line. . . . but if he lost count he could be an hour early or an hour late for meals!'*
(Jean Underdown – Colyton WI)

Mr F. Ham and Boxer, at Dartmouth carnival in the early 1960s. This was an annual event for 'dressed' horses and Mr Ham always won! He only stopped entering after a year when a freak electric storm caused his horse to bolt.
(Kath Edmunds – Dartmouth WI)

Mr Ernest Perry at Upcott Farm in 1960, using a horse-drawn rake. He had worked on the land since leaving school at 11. He had three horses to look after but this one knew the routine well and would start and stop without being told.
(Alice Rose – Broadhembury WI)

Above *Playtime at Huccombe school, 1966. The building is now used as a community centre.*
(Rosie Farleigh – Stokenham WI)

Left *In 1962 an old Shrove Tuesday custom was revived at Bridestowe. Local schoolchildren were taught the Lent Crocking song, which had been sung at the big houses locally by their forebears for food or pennies.*
(Iris Pearn – Bridestowe WI)

Right *A Hallowe'en procession round Stoke Gabriel was organised for the village children in 1979. After processing round the village there were games and refreshments in the village hall. This was before the introduction of 'Trick or Treat' as a traditional activity.*
(Eileen Wain – Stoke Gabriel WI)

Pancake day race at West Down, 1962. The event was held for 20 years, until 1972, and had begun as a Women's Institute group activity.
(Decima Jones – Heanton & Wrafton WI)

Beauty contests became very popular in the 1950s and 1960s – these were entrants for Miss Westward 1969, shown with presenter Keith Fordyce. 'The audience, comprising mainly sailors, did not agree with the results and booed the winners but cheered the losers, who were all well built compared to the girls who won!'
(Mollie Northway – Heavitree WI)

THE SIXTIES AND SEVENTIES (1960–1979)

Hauling in salmon fishing nets on the river Teign, 1970s.
(Sonia Gidal)

Totnes Show in the 1970s, a popular annual agricultural show held in July.
(Sonia Gidal)

Otter hounds at Harbertonford, 1970s. The Dartmoor Otter Hounds are now dispersed.
(Sonia Gidal)

Below *Totnes market, 1970s.*
(Sonia Gidal)

MODERN TIMES

(After 1980)

Much has changed but much has stayed the same. Today ships still meet with disaster along the Devon coastline. When the *Demetrios* foundered in 1992, one of seven recorded wrecks at Prawle Point, word quickly spread and an estimated 10,000 people came to view the wreckage in the following days. The road to East Prawle, the nearby village, had to be closed. It was a scene which, minus the cars, would have been familiar to Devon people of past centuries.

The Falklands War in 1982 was a reminder of Devon's close links with the armed forces. The Ministry of Defence has been one of the largest employers in the county, with half of the Royal Navy making its home here. The Army regularly uses Dartmoor for training exercises. After closing in 1974, RAF Chivenor reopened in 1980 as home to No 2 Tactical Weapons Unit.

Today the famous Devonport Dockyard is in private ownership. With the diminishing number of Service establishments and personnel, the city has diversified into service and high-tech industries and other manufacturing businesses.

Ships and boats are still built in Devon, at Appledore for instance, and Brixham is the county's largest fishing port, known as 'the mother of deep sea fisheries'. In 1986 it was the fourth largest port in England in terms of the catch landed. Fishing is of fundamental importance to the economy of the town and supports ancillary trades such as boat building and repairs, chandlers and gear makers.

Once the cidermakers Hill's in the south of the county and Inch's in Winkleigh in the north pretty well divided the county between them as far as sales were concerned, but Hill's no longer produces cider commercially and Inch's is no longer family-run, having been bought out by one of the big companies. Whiteways left its Whimple site in 1989, ending nearly a century of involvement in village life. There are very few, if any, large family cider-making businesses left in Devon now, and only about a dozen or so small ones.

The Tamar road bridge is sometimes not large enough to cope with today's holiday traffic, which increases year by year. The North Devon Link Route was designed, coming off the M5, to improve accessibility and control the flow of traffic to the northern resorts. On the A38, the 3,000 vehicles a day in 1938 had increased 50 years later to 23,000 a day and rising – and that did not include the peak summer flow. No confident solution has yet been proposed to a problem which afflicts not only Devon but every county in England.

Airports at Plymouth and Exeter connect the county with London and the Channel Islands. Though many of the old rail routes have been lost forever, enthusiasts have kept this older way of travel alive on some of the picturesque lines, such as the Dart Valley Railway and, in the north, the Tarka line.

Home life has changed beyond recognition over the century. Computers, videos and CDs are now commonplace in homes which 40 years ago would not have had a television

After 1980

set. Home ownership is now the norm rather than the exception; house prices rocketed during the 1980s, only to fall resoundingly. Shopping is now firmly based around the supermarket or shopping mall, but efforts are being made to bring people back to the town centres and village shops before it is too late to save them.

In 1990 the Devon Federation of WIs was 70 years old, and with the help of members' fundraising efforts a substantial contribution was made towards the National Trust's purchase of Wilsham Wood in North Devon. For the Federation's 75th birthday, Stover School in Newton Abbot was taken over for three days in July to demonstrate every facet of WI activity and sports.

Women's Institutes have been in the forefront of public opinion on every issue of importance since their foundation earlier this century. As we approach the millennium there are over 300 WIs in the county of Devon and we look forward to the challenges of the 21st century with a strong and enthusiastic membership.

The celebration of the 75th anniversary of the founding of the Women's Institute was marked by the passing of a banner around every WI in the county, moving from place to place by every conceivable form of transport. These Plymtree WI. members were arriving at Clyst Hydon WI. (Tiverton Gazette)

Left *The workers who cut the Dartmoor granite for the Falklands War Memorial. Stone from the Merrivale Quarry was chosen as the Royal Marines train on Dartmoor. This was a replacement – some of the original stones were badly damaged in a fire on board ship on their way to the Falklands.*
(Beryl Dark – Meavy & Sheepstor WI)

Storms can be a hazard inland as well as at sea – this 90 year old church lychgate was brought down by gales at Huntsham in 1990.
(Cissie Carpenter – Huntsham WI)

One of the last remaining small boat builders in Appledore H. Ford & Son, started in 1932. Amongst other things, they build the large ships' lifeboats, holding about 80 people. (Shirley Hocking – Appledore WI)

New ship Alphagas, *a gas carrier on her maiden voyage from Appledore, 1996. Appledore Shipbuilders Ltd were founded in 1855 and are equipped to build vessels up to 10,000 tonnes deadweight. As she left, Alphagas was skippered by a Dutch female captain Erzebet Warnik.* (Shirley Hocking – Appledore WI)

Left The wreck of the Demetrios *in 1992 off Prawle Point. En route for a breaker's yard, she broke her towline during a storm and was eventually dashed on to the rocks, where she broke in two. Her remains still lie strewn where she foundered.* (Cynthia Parke – Stokenham Evening WI)

Far left and left THEN & NOW: *Harvesting for cattle winter feed in the 1930s and 1996 – a horse-drawn grass cutter on Old Hill, Cullompton, and a modern 120hp tractor at Mutterton Dairy, Cullompton.* (Thelma Sheare – Kentisbeare WI)

THEN & NOW: Ploughing matches have pitted horse against machine over the past 50 years. **Opposite, Centre** *John Greenslade in the 1940s at Hayne Farm, Cheriton Fitzpaine.* **Opposite** *Cheriton Fitzpaine & District* *Ploughing Association celebrated its Jubilee in 1995.* **Above** *A ploughing match in 1995, overlooking Otterton, Colaton Raleigh.* (Olive Cheriton – Crediton WI; Elizabeth Furze – Cheriton Fitzpaine WI; Mrs Jean Underdown – Colyton WI)

Hill's operated their cider-making firm from Barkingdon Manor, Staverton, Totnes. Though it ceased manufacture in 1987, there is still a family-run farm. The family had been making cider for well over 100 years, with 100,000 gallons being made annually from locally grown cider apples.
(Mrs Irene Hill – Staverton WI)

Right *Turning the hay between the rows of bush cider apple trees at Whimple. Animals can no longer be grazed beneath the trees as they were in the traditional orchards.*
(Mary Burroughs – Whimple WI).

*Maypole dancers at Topsham First School, 1990s.
(Jean Binding – Topsham WI)*

Above *The Whimple Wassail was revived in January 1993, having not been performed since the 1930s. This ancient and well loved ceremony is said to 'wake up the trees ready for the next crop'.
(Mary Burrough – Whimple WI)*

MODERN TIMES (AFTER 1980)

Start of the Pancake Race, held every year, at Plymtree in 1995. The custom began in the 1970s, as a WI fundraiser, and is open to the whole village. (Wendy Evans – Plymtree WI)

What greater contrast could there be with the beginning of the century, than these ladies from Bradworthy WI preparing for the local carnival in 1996. (Ann Conway – Bradworthy WI)

Below The WI street party for the 50th anniversary of VE Day in may 1995 at Broadhempston. A 1940s-style dance was held in the village square with most people dressing up, followed by a firework display. Street parties still seem to be a popular way of marking important events.
(Edna Dowe – Broadhempston WI)